THE ASH-BORN WARRIORS

THE NAGA SADHUS AND THE SECRETS OF THE MAHA KUMBH

YS YADAV

Made with ♥ on the Notion Press Platform
www.notionpress.com

To the timeless protectors of truth,
The silent guardians of balance,
And to all those who walk the path of dharma,
This story is for you.

Contents

Disclaimer

This book is a fictional narrative interwoven with mythological, spiritual, and cultural elements drawn from Indian heritage and traditions. It is not intended to serve as an authoritative source on the subjects of Naga Sadhus, Maha Kumbh, or any associated rituals. Readers are advised to approach the content as creative storytelling rather than verified historical or religious accounts.

The author and publisher have taken great care to respect all spiritual and cultural practices mentioned in the book. Any errors, omissions, or interpretations are entirely unintended. The views expressed in the narrative are those of the characters and not reflective of the personal views or beliefs of the author or publisher.

By engaging with this book, readers acknowledge that it is a work of fiction and not a substitute for religious or historical texts.

Acknowledgements

This book would not have been possible without the guidance, inspiration, and unwavering support of those who believe in the power of stories to connect us with our roots and heritage.

First, I extend my heartfelt gratitude to the scholars, historians, and spiritual practitioners whose works and lives inspired this narrative. The richness of Indian mythology and the enigmatic traditions of the Naga Sadhus provided the foundation for this tale.

To my family, friends, and mentors, thank you for your encouragement, constructive feedback, and unwavering faith in my vision. Your support helped me overcome every challenge along the way.

I am deeply indebted to the vibrant and timeless tradition of the Maha Kumbh Mela, which stands as a testament to the resilience and unity of faith and culture.

Finally, to my readers, thank you for embarking on this journey with me. May this story inspire curiosity, reflection, and a deeper appreciation for the mysteries of the universe.

Foreword

The **Maha Kumbh Mela** is not just a gathering; it is an intersection of faith, culture, and cosmic energy. It represents the eternal rhythm of the universe, a confluence of past, present, and future. Within its sacred rituals and mystic traditions lies a tapestry of untold stories, stories that connect humanity to something far greater than itself.

The *Ash-Born Warriors* seeks to unveil one such story, exploring the lives of the enigmatic Naga Sadhus, their connection to the divine Sudarshana Chakra, and their eternal duty to preserve balance in an ever-changing world.

This narrative is not merely a work of fiction but a tribute to the enduring legacy of *Sanatana Dharma* and the unseen forces that uphold it. It is a story of sacrifice, courage, and unwavering faith in the cosmic order, a story that reminds us that even in the darkest of times, dharma will always find its protectors.

As you turn these pages, you will journey into a world of mystery and spirituality, where the boundaries between myth and reality blur. I hope this book inspires you to reflect on the deeper truths that govern our existence and the eternal quest for balance.

Let us honor the unseen, the unknown, and the untold.

With gratitude,

YS Yadav

Preface

The realms of myth, spirituality, and devotion often exist in a space beyond our complete comprehension. Whispered through generations, some stories echo with familiar resonance, while others remain veiled in enigma, awaiting discovery. The Ash-Born Warriors endeavors to illuminate one such untold narrative, deeply rooted in India's rich spiritual tapestry and woven with the enduring threads of faith, sacrifice, and unwavering vigilance.

The Maha Kumbh Mela, the largest spiritual gathering on Earth, is an experience of unparalleled grandeur. It transcends the mere definition of an event; it is a vibrant confluence of energies, a rare alignment of celestial and terrestrial forces. Amidst the millions who converge there, the enigmatic Naga Sadhus command attention. These ash-smeared ascetics, with their fearless demeanor and resolute spirit, are not simply custodians of ancient traditions; they are the silent warriors of Sanatana Dharma, their very existence embodying age-old secrets and a purpose that transcends ordinary understanding.

This book draws from the deep wellspring of Indian mythology, history, and spirituality, exploring the fascinating intersection of fact and fiction. At the heart of this narrative lies the Sudarshana Chakra, a potent cosmic symbol of balance and dharma, entrusted to the Naga Sadhus themselves by Adi Shankaracharya. What unfolds is a journey through time, revealing the profound sacrifices of these guardians, their timeless duty to protect, and the intricate mysteries that bind them to the very fabric of the universe.

The Ash-Born Warriors is not intended as a historical document or a religious treatise. Rather, it is a story—a tribute to the unseen and the unknown, an homage to those who stand as eternal protectors of truth. It is a carefully crafted exploration of the mystical, the spiritual, and the profound, approached with reverence and a deep respect for the traditions it seeks to portray.

As you embark on this journey, I invite you to look beyond the surface, to question the often-blurred boundaries between myth and reality, and to contemplate the delicate equilibrium that sustains life as we know it. This story is for the curious minds, the seekers of wisdom, and the dreamers who dare to imagine. It is, ultimately, a story for you.

With reverence and gratitude,

YS Yadav

Author

Prologue

The Silent Flame

High in the snow-clad Himalayas, where time seemed to dissolve into silence, a sacred fire flickered in the depths of a hidden cave. The flames illuminated a gathering of ash-smeared figures seated in perfect stillness, their dreadlocked hair trailing like serpents coiled in meditation. These were the Naga Sadhus, warriors of spirituality, bound not by blood or creed but by vows older than memory.

The air vibrated with the hum of a chant, a rhythm that seemed to pulse with the very heartbeat of the universe:

"Shankaram Shankaracharyam Keshavam."

At the head of the assembly sat Acharya Dharmendra, his body unmoving, his eyes closed in profound focus. Around him, the Sadhus formed a perfect circle, each emanating a stillness that bordered on the divine. Among them was Rudranath, the youngest of their brotherhood, his youthful energy tempered by the gravity of his initiation.

Acharya Dharmendra finally spoke, his voice deep and resonant, carrying the weight of centuries.

"The Maha Kumbh Mela draws near," he began, his eyes still closed. "The Sangam's waters will shimmer with the celestial alignments, drawing millions to its shores. But amidst the seekers of light, there will be shadows. Forces of adharma will rise, seeking to disturb the balance of this age."

The Sadhus remained silent, their faces impassive, but the fire seemed to crackle louder in the stillness, as though it, too, understood the weight of his words.

"Our task is unchanged," the Acharya continued. "Since the time of Adi Shankaracharya, we have safeguarded the eternal truths of Sanatana Dharma. We are its warriors, its protectors, its silent flame. But this Kumbh carries a greater danger. The balance itself is threatened."

Rudranath, unable to contain his curiosity, leaned forward. "Acharya, what is this danger? What are we to protect?"

The Acharya opened his eyes, his gaze piercing and calm. "Not all truths are spoken, Rudranath. Some are carried in silence, guarded in shadows. You will know when the time comes."

Another Sadhu, older and more weathered, spoke softly. *"The balance of Sanatana Dharma is fragile in this age of Kaliyuga. What we guard must not fall into the hands of those who would misuse its power. Even a whisper of it in the wrong ear could bring destruction."*

Rudranath sat back, his heart heavy but resolute. He had chosen this path, renouncing the world and its attachments. Whatever lay ahead, he would face it as a guardian of dharma.

The Acharya rose, his figure towering against the glow of the fire. *"The wheel of time turns, and we must ensure it turns toward righteousness. Prepare yourselves. The Maha Kumbh is not merely a festival, it is a battlefield."*

As the Acharya's voice faded, the chant resumed, rising and falling like the tides of eternity:

"Shankaram Shankaracharyam Keshavam."

CHAPTER ONE

Meera's Arrival

The train screeched to a halt at Prayagraj Station, and **Meera Desai** stepped onto the crowded platform, her senses immediately overwhelmed by the chaos of the Maha Kumbh Mela. The air was thick with the scent of burning incense and the distant hum of prayers. Pilgrims flowed in every direction, their faces alive with devotion, their hands clutching flowers, brass vessels, and small earthen lamps.

Meera adjusted her bag and clutched her camera tightly. This was her first assignment outside the newsroom in months, and she wasn't sure if she was excited or apprehensive. The Maha Kumbh was said to be the largest spiritual gathering on earth, a spectacle of faith, hope, and redemption. But she wasn't here to document rituals or photograph the throngs of people seeking salvation in the waters of the Sangam.

Meera was after something far more elusive: the **Naga Sadhus**.

For weeks, she had been poring over articles and historical accounts of these mysterious ascetics. They appeared like phantoms during the Kumbh, their bodies smeared with ash, their dreadlocks flowing like wild rivers, and their tridents gleaming under the sun. The Nagas were warriors of **Sanatana Dharma**, protectors of an ancient order, or so the legends claimed. But no one knew much about them beyond the myths.

A World of Chaos and Devotion

As she exited the station, Meera was met with a sea of people. Pilgrims sang bhajans in unison, children ran barefoot carrying garlands, and vendors shouted over the din, selling everything from clay pots to rudraksha beads. The energy was palpable, something ancient and primal seemed to hum beneath the surface of the chaos.

She flagged down a rickshaw and gave the driver instructions to take her to the Akhadas, the camps of the ascetics. "The Nagas are there," she said, and the driver gave her a knowing glance.

"They don't speak much to outsiders," he said as he pedaled through the narrow streets. "You'll be lucky if they even acknowledge you."

"I'm not here to make friends," Meera replied, though she couldn't help but feel a pang of doubt. Would she even get close to them? Or would they dismiss her as yet another curious observer, poking her nose into things she didn't understand?

The First Hints of Mystery

As the rickshaw made its way toward the Akhadas, Meera noticed a small group of pilgrims huddled by a tea stall. They were whispering in hushed voices, their faces etched with unease.

"Three men vanished last night," one of them said, his voice barely audible. "They were last seen near the Sangam."

"They say strange lights have been appearing," another added. "It's an omen."

Meera leaned closer, her journalist's instincts kicking in. "What kind of lights?" she asked.

The men turned to her, startled by her sudden intrusion. One of them, an older man with a weathered face, shook his head. "It's nothing you need to worry about. Just focus on your prayers."

But Meera couldn't shake the feeling that there was more to their whispers than mere superstition. She made a mental note to investigate further.

The Naga Akhada

The Akhadas were unlike anything Meera had imagined. Rows of tents lined the sprawling grounds, their entrances adorned with tridents and saffron flags fluttering in the breeze. Fires burned in clay pits, sending spirals of smoke into the air, and ash-covered ascetics moved silently among them, their eyes piercing, their movements deliberate.

Meera hesitated at the entrance, suddenly feeling out of place. She was just a journalist with a camera and a notebook, what right did she have to enter this sacred space?

Before she could turn back, a voice called out to her. "Who are you?"

She turned to see a young Sadhu standing nearby, his body smeared with ash, a rudraksha mala hanging around his neck. His gaze was intense but not unkind.

"My name is Meera Desai," she said, holding up her press badge. "I'm a journalist. I want to understand your world."

The Sadhu studied her for a long moment before nodding. "Come."

Swami Shivananda

The young Sadhu led her to the central fire, where an older ascetic sat cross-legged, his body still as stone. His aura was commanding, his presence radiating an unshakable calm. This was Swami Shivananda, one of the elder Nagas.

The young Sadhu bowed slightly and said, "Swami-ji, this woman seeks knowledge of our ways."

Shivananda opened his eyes and looked at Meera. His gaze was piercing, as though he could see straight into her soul. "Knowledge is not given freely," he said after a moment. "It must be earned. Why have you come here?"

Meera swallowed her nervousness. "I've read about the Naga Sadhus, their history, their rituals. But no one seems to know who you really are or what you protect. I want to tell your story."

Shivananda's lips curved into a faint smile. "Our story is not one that can be told. It is one that must be lived. But you may observe. Perhaps, in time, you will understand."

A Night in the Akhada

That night, Meera stayed in the Akhada, her notebook and camera lying forgotten beside her as she watched the Sadhus go about their rituals. They moved with a sense of purpose, their chants echoing through the camp like the beating of a drum.

She noticed something strange, despite their outward calm, there was a tension in the air, as though the Sadhus were preparing for something. She overheard fragments of conversations:

"The signs are becoming clearer." "We must be vigilant." "The balance must not be disturbed."

Meera tried to piece together what they were talking about, but no one offered her any explanations. She felt like an outsider looking in on a world she couldn't fully comprehend.

As she drifted off to sleep, the chants of the Nagas echoed in her mind. There was something they were protecting, something greater than she could imagine. But what?

CHAPTER TWO

Guardians of Sanatana Dharma

The next morning, Meera woke to the sound of conch shells and the rhythmic hum of chants. The camp was already alive with activity, but amidst the commotion, the Sadhus moved with a quiet discipline. They weren't like the wandering ascetics she had imagined, they seemed organized, almost militaristic.

As she stepped outside, she noticed Swami Shivananda seated by the fire, surrounded by a few younger Sadhus. His posture was regal, his presence commanding. Meera hesitated, unsure if she should interrupt, but the Swami gestured for her to sit.

"You have questions," he said, his voice calm yet firm.

Meera nodded. "I've read about the Nagas, but no one seems to know much about your origins. Who are you really? And why do you call yourselves warriors of Sanatana Dharma?"

Swami Shivananda's eyes glinted with something between amusement and reverence. "To understand the Nagas, you must first understand Sanatana Dharma."

The Origin of the Nagas

Swami Shivananda began his story, his voice resonant like the tolling of a temple bell.

"In the early centuries of Kaliyuga, as the cycles of dharma began to waver, a great soul descended to restore balance. His name was Adi Shankaracharya. He traveled across Bharat, reviving the Vedic traditions and unifying the fragmented spiritual paths under the banner of Sanatana Dharma.

"But Shankaracharya, in his wisdom, knew that philosophy alone could not preserve the eternal order. Spirituality needed warriors, those who could defend dharma when it was under threat. And so, he established the Dashanami Sampradaya, dividing it into ten orders of ascetics, each with a distinct role. Among them were the Nagas, the warriors of dharma."

Meera leaned forward, captivated. "Warriors? What kind of warriors?"

Shivananda smiled faintly. "Not warriors of conquest, but warriors of protection. While others meditated in caves and ashrams, the Nagas took up arms to defend temples, scriptures, and sacred sites. They trained in martial arts, wielded weapons, and fought not for power but to preserve the sanctity of dharma."

The Nagas and India's Struggles

The Swami's voice grew heavier as he recounted the Nagas' role in India's history.

"When invaders came to this land, seeking to destroy its temples and suppress its wisdom, the Nagas rose to meet them. During the Mughal invasions, it was the Nagas who guarded the temples of Kashi, Mathura, and Prayagraj.

"There is a story," he continued, his eyes distant, "of the time when Aurangzeb ordered the desecration of Prayagraj. His soldiers marched toward the sacred Sangam, determined to destroy the temples that stood there. The Nagas, armed only with tridents, confronted them. Their chants of 'Shankaram Shankaracharyam Keshavam' echoed across the battlefield, and though they were outnumbered, their resolve was unshakable. They fought not for victory but for dharma, and their sacrifice preserved the sanctity of the land."

Meera listened, her heart pounding. These weren't just ascetics, they were guardians of a spiritual legacy that spanned millennia.

Hints of a Deeper Mission

"But Swami-ji," Meera ventured, "that was centuries ago. What do the Nagas protect now? Surely, there's no need for warriors in this age?"

Shivananda's expression darkened slightly. "Kaliyuga is an age of illusions, where adharma wears many faces. The battles we fight now are not always visible, but they are no less real."

He paused, as if weighing his words carefully. "There are forces in this world that seek to unravel the fabric of dharma. The Nagas exist to ensure that balance is maintained. What we protect is not just tradition, it is the very essence of cosmic order."

Meera frowned. "What do you mean by 'cosmic order'? Is it something tangible, or are you speaking metaphorically?"

The Swami gave her a measured look. "Some truths cannot be explained, they must be experienced. You will understand in time."

The Philosophy of Dharma

As the fire crackled between them, Shivananda shifted his focus to the teachings of Sanatana Dharma.

"Dharma," he explained, "is not just a set of rules. It is the natural order of the universe, the balance that sustains life. The Vedas describe it as 'Ritam,' the rhythm of existence. To follow dharma is to align oneself with that rhythm, to live in harmony with the cosmos."

He quoted a verse from the Bhagavad Gita:

> *"Whenever there is a decline in righteousness and a rise in unrighteousness, I manifest Myself to protect the good, destroy the wicked, and re-establish dharma."*

Meera nodded slowly, trying to absorb the enormity of what he was saying. "And the Nagas see themselves as part of that cycle?"

"Not just part of it," Shivananda corrected. "We are its guardians. Our duty is not to impose dharma but to preserve it. And sometimes, preservation requires great sacrifice."

A Cryptic Warning

Before Meera could ask more, a younger Sadhu approached, his face grave. "Swami-ji," he said softly, "there has been another incident near the Sangam. A pilgrim reported seeing symbols carved into the sand, similar to the ones we found earlier."

Shivananda's expression grew tense. "And the lights?"

"They've been reported again, near the forest."

Meera watched as the Sadhus exchanged glances, their earlier calm replaced by a sense of urgency. Shivananda rose, turning to Rudranath. "Double the watch at the perimeter. We cannot allow them to move closer."

Meera stood as well, her curiosity now mingled with unease. "What's happening? What symbols? Who are you watching for?"

Shivananda looked at her, his gaze unreadable. "There are forces here that do not come for salvation. Remember what I told you, Kaliyuga wears many faces. Not all who gather at the Kumbh come with pure intentions."

With that, he turned and walked away, leaving Meera standing by the fire, her mind racing with questions. What were they guarding? And who, or what, was trying to take it?

CHAPTER THREE

Shadows in the Mela

The campfires of the Akhadas burned low as the first light of dawn kissed the horizon, yet the air around the Maha Kumbh was charged with an unsettling energy. Meera walked along the riverbank, her camera slung around her neck, her mind still spinning from Swami Shivananda's cryptic warnings the night before. Something was stirring beneath the surface of the world's largest spiritual gathering, and she was determined to uncover it.

Pilgrims were already gathering at the Triveni Sangam, the confluence of the Ganga, Yamuna, and Saraswati. Their prayers rose with the mist, voices mingling with the cries of priests and the rhythmic clang of temple bells. But amidst the devotion, Meera sensed an undercurrent of unease, an invisible thread of tension that seemed to weave through the crowd.

The Symbols and the Lights

She noticed a group of villagers gathered near the water's edge, their faces drawn and anxious. Intrigued, she approached cautiously, catching snippets of their conversation.

"They found another one this morning," an old woman murmured. "Near the Sangam."

"A bad omen," a man replied, shaking his head. "The last time this happened, people disappeared."

"What did they find?" Meera asked, stepping closer.

The group turned to her, their eyes wary. After a long pause, the old woman spoke. "Symbols. Carved into the sand by the river. No one knows what they mean, but they're not natural."

"And the lights?" Meera pressed.

The woman hesitated, then nodded. "They come at night. Strange, flickering lights near the forest. They say it's the work of dark forces."

Meera's heart quickened. This was no coincidence, these were the same lights the Nagas had spoken of. But what did they mean? And who was behind them?

The Disappearance

Later that day, as Meera wandered through the bustling Mela, the air was thick with rumors of a disappearance. A young pilgrim, barely twenty, had gone missing the night before, his last known location near the Sangam. His family was frantic, their cries echoing through the crowd.

Meera found herself drawn to the scene, her journalist's instincts sharpening. "Have there been other disappearances?" she asked a bystander.

The man nodded grimly. "Three in the past week. All near the river."

"And no one has seen anything?" Meera asked, incredulous.

The man shook his head. "The Nagas know something. They've been patrolling the area every night."

A Tense Encounter

That evening, Meera returned to the Naga Akhada. The camp was quieter than usual, its usual hum of chants replaced by an air of vigilance. She spotted Rudranath standing near the perimeter, his trident resting against his shoulder.

"You've been watching the river," she said, approaching him. "Why?"

Rudranath glanced at her but said nothing. His eyes scanned the horizon, ever watchful.

"Is it about the symbols? The lights?" Meera pressed. "You know something, don't you?"

He sighed, his shoulders tense. "There are forces at work here that you don't understand. This is not just a festival, Meera. It's a battlefield."

"A battlefield for what?" she asked.

"For balance," he replied. "For dharma. And not all battles are fought with weapons."

The Ritual of Protection

That night, Meera was invited to witness a ritual at the heart of the Akhada. The Nagas gathered around a massive fire, their chants rising in unison, their voices deep and resonant. The air seemed to vibrate with their energy, the flames dancing higher as the ritual intensified.

Swami Shivananda stood at the center, his arms raised as he invoked an ancient mantra:

> *"Pratibhatsreni Bhishana*
> *Vargunasthoma Bhushana*
> *Jyanibhayasthan Kartana*
> *Jagadavasthan Kartana..."*

The Sudarshana Ashtakam echoed through the camp, its verses imbued with a power Meera could feel in her very bones. The ritual seemed to create an invisible barrier, a shield against the unseen forces that threatened the Mela.

"What are they protecting?" Meera wondered aloud.

Rudranath, standing beside her, answered softly. "The same thing we've always protected. The balance of Sanatana Dharma."

The First Glimpse of the Enemy

As the ritual ended, a commotion erupted at the edge of the camp. Meera followed Rudranath to the source of the noise, her heart pounding. A group of Nagas had discovered a man skulking near the perimeter, his face hidden beneath a hood.

"He's not one of us," one of the Sadhus said, his voice low and dangerous.

The man refused to speak, his eyes darting around nervously. But when the Nagas pulled back his hood, Meera gasped. His forehead bore the same cryptic symbols that had been found near the Sangam.

Swami Shivananda stepped forward, his gaze piercing. "Who sent you?" he demanded.

The man remained silent, but his body trembled as though he were caught in the grip of some unseen force. Finally, he muttered a single word: "Aghoris."

The Shadow of the Aghoris

The name sent a ripple of unease through the Nagas. Meera had read about the Aghoris, ascetics who lived on the fringes of society, embracing death and darkness in their quest for liberation. But why would they infiltrate the Kumbh? And what did they want?

Swami Shivananda turned to his brothers, his voice calm but resolute. "This is no longer a matter of vigilance. The Aghoris seek something they must not have. We cannot let them disrupt the balance."

Rudranath stepped forward. "What do they want, Acharya?"

Shivananda's gaze darkened. "Something far greater than they can comprehend. And if they find it, the consequences will be catastrophic."

Closing Suspense

As the Nagas prepared for what lay ahead, Meera felt the weight of their mission pressing down on her. The symbols, the lights, the disappearances, it was all connected. But connected to what?

That night, as she lay awake in her tent, the wind carried the echoes of the Nagas' chants. She couldn't shake the feeling that something immense and dangerous was about to unfold, and she was standing at the heart of it.

CHAPTER FOUR

The Hidden Purpose

The night sky over Prayagraj was a tapestry of stars, but Meera felt no peace as she walked along the dimly lit paths of the Akhada. The air was heavy with anticipation, the kind that precedes a storm. The Nagas moved with a quiet urgency, their eyes scanning the darkness as though expecting an unseen enemy.

Earlier that evening, the captured man had been taken away, his cryptic mutterings silenced by Swami Shivananda's commanding presence. But his single utterance, Aghoris, echoed in Meera's mind, a puzzle piece that refused to fit.

She found Rudranath near the central fire, his trident resting against a log. He looked up as she approached, his expression unreadable.

"They're coming, aren't they?" she asked, her voice low.

He nodded. "The Aghoris do not gather without purpose. And their purpose is never light."

The Philosophy of the Aghoris

Meera sat down beside Rudranath, the flickering firelight casting shadows on their faces. "I thought the Aghoris were ascetics, like you. Aren't they just... another sect?"

Rudranath's jaw tightened. "The Aghoris are seekers of liberation, but their path diverged from Sanatana Dharma long ago. They believe in breaking every taboo, every boundary, to transcend the illusion of the material world. But some among them have turned that quest into a hunger for power."

"Power?" Meera frowned. "What kind of power?"

He hesitated, then glanced toward the tent where Swami Shivananda was meditating. "They believe the Kumbh's celestial alignment amplifies the energies of this land. And there is... something here they seek to control."

Meera leaned closer. "What is it?"

Rudranath didn't answer. Instead, he stared into the fire, his face shadowed by doubt. "Some truths are better left hidden."

A Meeting of Elders

Inside the main tent, Swami Shivananda sat in council with the elder Nagas. Their voices were low, but the tension was palpable.

"They are not here by chance," one of the elders said. "The symbols near the Sangam, the lights, the disappearances, it all points to a ritual."

"And they know what they're looking for," another added. "If they reach it, "

"They won't," Shivananda interrupted, his voice firm. "The Sudarshana Chakra has remained hidden for centuries. It is not theirs to find."

Meera, standing just outside the tent, froze. The words hung in the air like a revelation. The **Sudarshana Chakra.** She had read about it in mythological texts, a divine weapon of unimaginable power, wielded by Lord Vishnu himself. But why were the Nagas talking about it as though it were real?

She took a step closer, straining to hear.

"The Chakra is not just a weapon," Shivananda continued. "It is the embodiment of dharma, a force of creation and destruction. If it falls into the wrong hands, it could unmake the balance of this age."

"And the Aghoris?" one of the elders asked.

"They believe they can harness its power to rewrite the cycle of time. But they do not understand that the Chakra does not serve ambition. It serves dharma."

The Aghoris' Plan

That night, as Meera sat in her tent, her thoughts raced. The Sudarshana Chakra was no longer just a myth, it was real, and it was here. But why was it hidden? And why did the Nagas guard it with such secrecy?

She couldn't sleep. The weight of the revelation pressed down on her, and with it came a growing fear. If the Aghoris truly sought the Chakra, what would they do if they found it?

Meanwhile, in a shadowy grove near the forest's edge, the Aghoris were gathering. Their leader, a towering figure with coal-black eyes, stood before a stone altar, his voice low and menacing.

"The Chakra is here," he said, his words a hiss. "Its energy is woven into the very fabric of this land. But the Nagas guard it, as they have for centuries."

He raised his hand, revealing a strange amulet etched with the same symbols found near the Sangam. "We will break their barriers. The alignment of the Kumbh will amplify the energy of the Chakra, and when the time is right, we will claim it."

His followers chanted in unison, their voices rising into the night: "Adharma must rise, and the cycle must end."

Meera Confronts Shivananda

The next morning, Meera confronted Swami Shivananda. She couldn't keep quiet any longer.

"Swami-ji," she began, her voice steady but insistent, "I overheard your conversation last night. You spoke about the Sudarshana Chakra. I thought it was just a myth, a story from the epics. But it's real, isn't it?"

Shivananda regarded her calmly. "You have a sharp mind, Meera. But not all knowledge is meant to be uncovered."

"Why are you keeping it a secret?" she pressed. "If the Aghoris are trying to find it, why not tell the world? Why not protect it openly?"

"Because power corrupts," Shivananda said, his voice firm. "The Sudarshana Chakra is not a treasure to be displayed. It is a force of dharma, and only those aligned with the eternal order can wield it. To reveal it is to invite chaos."

Meera's frustration bubbled to the surface. "But if it's so important, why not destroy it? Why let it exist at all?"

The Swami's expression softened. "Because the Chakra is not just a weapon, it is the wheel of time, the embodiment of balance. To destroy it would be to destroy the universe itself."

A Growing Threat

That evening, the Nagas doubled their patrols. The Aghoris were growing bolder, their presence felt in every corner of the Mela. Pilgrims whispered of strange occurrences, shadows moving in the forest, whispers in the wind, and lights that flickered like fireflies but carried an unnatural glow.

Meera followed Rudranath to the edge of the camp, her camera in hand. "Do you really think they'll come tonight?" she asked.

"They're already here," he replied, his voice grim. "We're just waiting for them to show themselves."

As the sun dipped below the horizon, the air grew colder. The Nagas stood in silent formation, their tridents gleaming in the moonlight. And in the distance, the faint sound of drums echoed through the forest.

The battle for the Sudarshana Chakra had begun.

CHAPTER FIVE

The Sudarshana Chakra Revealed

The fire at the heart of the Naga Akhada burned with an intensity that seemed to transcend the physical. The air was thick with reverence, and the chanting of the Sudarshana Ashtakam had created an almost tangible vibration, as though the very cosmos were leaning in to listen.

Meera sat cross-legged near the fire, her pulse quickened by the magnitude of what she had just learned. The Sudarshana Chakra, a mythical weapon of Lord Vishnu, the wheel of cosmic order, was real. And it was here, hidden among these ascetics. But how? And why?

Swami Shivananda's voice broke through her thoughts, deep and resonant. "The story of the Sudarshana Chakra is the story of Sanatana Dharma itself. To understand why it is here, you must understand where it has been."

The Birth of the Chakra: Satya Yuga

"In the beginning, there was Vishnu," Shivananda began, his voice low but commanding. "He who preserves the balance of creation, who holds the universe in his infinite grace. From his essence was born the Sudarshana Chakra, a manifestation of cosmic order. It was forged not by mortal hands but by the divine energy of creation itself."

He paused, his gaze fixed on the fire as though seeing the past unfold within its flames. "The Vedas speak of the Chakra as Ritam, the truth that binds existence. In the Satya Yuga, the age of perfection, it spun silently at the heart of the cosmos, ensuring that dharma prevailed."

Shivananda quoted from the Rig Veda:

"*Ritam cha satyam cha abhiddhat tapaso adhyajaayata.*"

(From cosmic truth and order, creation was born.)

"The Chakra was not a weapon in those times," he continued. "It was a symbol of harmony, untouched by conflict. But as the Yugas turned, as the purity of the world diminished, the Chakra's role began to shift."

The Treta Yuga: Rama's Invocation

"In the Treta Yuga," Shivananda said, "the world faced its first great test of dharma. Ravana, the king of Lanka, rose to power through arrogance and unchecked ambition. His tyranny spread across the land, and the balance of creation began to falter."

Meera frowned. "But wasn't Ravana defeated by Lord Rama's arrow? What role did the Chakra play?"

Shivananda smiled faintly, as though expecting the question. "You are correct, Ravana was slain by the Brahmastra, not the Chakra. But before the great battle, Lord Rama performed the Sudarshana Homa, an ancient ritual invoking the blessings of the Chakra."

Meera's curiosity deepened. "Why?"

"Because defeating Ravana was not just a physical battle, it was a spiritual one," Shivananda explained. "The Sudarshana Chakra represents the wheel of time, the force that ensures dharma triumphs over adharma. Rama understood that to prevail, he needed more than strength; he needed alignment with the cosmic order. The Homa brought him the clarity and divine guidance he needed to fulfill his mission."

Shivananda quoted from the Ramayana:

"Dharma eva hato hanti, dharmo rakshati rakshitah."

(Dharma destroys those who violate it; dharma protects those who uphold it.)

"The Chakra did not strike Ravana," he continued, "but its presence ensured that dharma prevailed. It illuminated the path for Rama, guiding him to victory."

The Dwapara Yuga: Krishna's Wielder

"As the world entered the Dwapara Yuga," Shivananda said, "the lines between dharma and adharma blurred further. It was an age of moral complexity, where even the righteous found themselves tested. In this era, the Sudarshana Chakra came into the hands of Lord Krishna."

Meera's mind filled with images of Krishna, the divine strategist. "He used it as a weapon, didn't he?"

"Yes," Shivananda replied. "But Krishna's use of the Chakra was always purposeful, never reckless. It was with the Chakra that he saved Draupadi's honor in the court of Hastinapura, that he ended Shishupala's arrogance, and that he guided the Pandavas in the Kurukshetra war."

Shivananda's voice grew softer. "But even Krishna wielded the Chakra sparingly. He understood its power, its responsibility. To wield the Sudarshana Chakra is to hold the balance of the cosmos in your hands. It is not a burden to be taken lightly."

The Kaliyuga: Adi Shankaracharya and the Naga Sadhus

Meera leaned forward, her heart pounding. "But how did it come to the Nagas? And why is it here now?"

Shivananda's expression grew solemn. "That story begins in the early centuries of Kaliyuga, when the light of dharma began to flicker. Temples were desecrated, scriptures were burned, and humanity's understanding of the divine began to waver. It was during this time that Adi Shankaracharya was born, a child of divine will, sent to restore the balance."

Meera nodded, recalling the fragments of history she had studied. "He unified the paths of dharma, didn't he? The Dashanami Sampradaya?"

"Yes," Shivananda said. "But his mission went beyond philosophy. During his travels, Shankaracharya reached the sacred city of Badrinath, where he entered deep meditation. It is said that while he meditated, Lord Vishnu appeared before him. Vishnu, foreseeing the challenges of Kaliyuga, entrusted Shankaracharya with the Sudarshana Chakra."

He paused, his voice reverent. "Shankaracharya understood the gravity of this gift. He knew the Chakra could not remain unguarded in an age where adharma wore many faces. And so, he entrusted it to the Naga Sadhus."

The Nagas' Mandate

Shivananda's gaze burned with intensity. "The Nagas are not ordinary ascetics. Shankaracharya created us to be warriors of dharma, protectors of the cosmic balance. He gave us a mandate: to guard the Chakra with our lives, to keep it hidden from those who would misuse its power, and to act only when dharma itself is at risk."

Meera's voice trembled. "What did he tell you about its power?"

Shivananda's voice lowered. "He warned us: 'The Chakra is not a weapon for ambition. It answers only to dharma. If ever it is wielded for selfish purposes, it will bring destruction, not to the world, but to the one who wields it.'"

The Aghoris' Threat

Rudranath, who had been silent until now, spoke. "And that is why the Aghoris must be stopped. They believe they can use the Chakra to end the cycle of creation and destruction, but they do not understand its purpose. The Chakra does not serve adharma."

Shivananda nodded. "If the Aghoris succeed, they will unmake the balance of the universe. There will be no creation, no preservation, no destruction. Only chaos."

A Call to Action

As the fire crackled and the chanting of the Nagas resumed, Meera felt the weight of the story pressing down on her. The Sudarshana Chakra was not just a relic, it was the key to the survival of Sanatana Dharma. And now, its fate rested in the hands of these ascetics.

Swami Shivananda rose, his eyes blazing with resolve. "The Aghoris have begun their ritual. We must act now, or all will be lost."

The Nagas moved into formation, their tridents gleaming in the firelight. Meera followed, her heart pounding. She didn't know what lay ahead, but one thing was certain: the battle for the Sudarshana Chakra had begun.

CHAPTER SIX

Battle Beneath the Stars

The forest surrounding the Maha Kumbh Mela seemed alive with an unsettling energy as the night deepened. Shadows flickered like living things, and the air felt charged, heavy with the weight of ancient forces stirring. The chants of the Aghoris echoed faintly in the distance, their dark ritual weaving a sinister thread into the fabric of the night.

At the edge of the Naga camp, Swami Shivananda stood with Rudranath and the other Sadhus, their tridents glinting in the moonlight. Meera lingered behind them, her heart pounding. The Nagas had transformed from serene ascetics into warriors, their resolve etched into their ash-smeared faces.

"They have crossed the threshold," Shivananda said, his voice low but resolute. "The Aghoris have begun their attempt to corrupt the Sangam's energy. If they succeed, the balance of this age will be shattered."

Rudranath tightened his grip on his trident. "We won't let that happen."

The Aghoris' Ritual

Deep in the heart of the forest, the Aghoris had gathered around a massive stone altar carved with ancient symbols. Their leader, a towering figure draped in black, stood at its center, his hands raised to the sky. Around him, his followers chanted in a guttural language, their voices weaving an eerie harmony with the crackling flames of their fire.

"The Chakra's energy resonates here," the leader intoned, his voice thick with malice. "The alignment of the stars amplifies its power. Tonight, we will claim it and break the cycle of time itself."

He raised an amulet inscribed with the same cryptic symbols that had appeared near the Sangam. As he chanted, a dark energy began to pulse from the altar, spreading outward in ripples that made the very air tremble.

The Nagas Advance

Swami Shivananda led the Nagas through the forest, their movements silent and precise. Meera followed, her heart hammering in her chest. She had never seen anything like this, a group of ascetics moving with the discipline of an army, their eyes burning with unshakable determination.

"The Aghoris are blinded by their ambition," Shivananda said quietly as they approached the clearing. "They believe they can control the Chakra's energy, but they do not understand its nature. The Chakra answers only to dharma. It will not bend to their will."

As they neared the Aghori camp, the ground seemed to hum with an unnatural energy. Meera felt a wave of nausea wash over her, but she pressed on, determined to see this through.

The Confrontation

The Nagas emerged from the shadows, their formation tight, their tridents raised. The Aghori leader turned to face them, his coal-black eyes gleaming with a mixture of rage and triumph.

"So, the guardians have come," he sneered. "Did you think your chants and rituals could stop us? We are the breakers of chains, the heralds of a new order. The Chakra will be ours."

Swami Shivananda stepped forward, his voice calm but commanding. "You do not understand what you seek. The Sudarshana Chakra is not a tool for ambition. It is the embodiment of balance. To wield it without alignment to dharma is to destroy yourself."

The leader laughed, a harsh, grating sound. "Balance? Dharma? These are the lies of a world afraid to evolve. The Chakra's power will free us from the shackles of creation and destruction. With it, we will remake the universe."

The Battle

The air seemed to crackle with energy as the two groups clashed. The Nagas moved with precision, their tridents flashing in the firelight as they parried the Aghoris' crude weapons. Rudranath fought with a ferocity Meera hadn't seen before, his movements fluid and purposeful.

The Aghoris, however, were relentless. Their dark chants seemed to fuel their strength, and their leader stood at the center of the chaos, his hands raised as he continued his incantations.

Meera watched from the edge of the clearing, her heart in her throat. The battle was not just physical, it was spiritual, a clash of philosophies and energies. The Nagas fought to preserve balance, while the Aghoris sought to unmake it.

The Sudarshana Chakra Awakens

As the battle raged on, a blinding light suddenly erupted from the center of the clearing. Both groups froze as the light grew brighter, illuminating the forest in an otherworldly glow. The Sudarshana Chakra had awakened.

It hovered above the altar, spinning slowly, its golden edges gleaming with an intensity that seemed to pierce through time itself. The Aghori leader reached out toward it, his face alight with greed.

But as his fingers grazed the edge of the Chakra, a searing energy shot through him. He screamed, his body convulsing as the Chakra's power overwhelmed him. The Nagas stood silently, their heads bowed in reverence, as the light of the Chakra filled the clearing.

The Chakra's Judgment

The Chakra spun faster, its energy pulsing outward in waves that seemed to cleanse the very air. The Aghori leader fell to his knees, his body trembling as the light consumed him. One by one, his followers dropped their weapons, their chants faltering as the Chakra's power shattered their resolve.

Swami Shivananda stepped forward, his voice steady. "The Sudarshana Chakra does not serve ambition. It serves dharma. And dharma has no place for those who seek to unmake it."

The light of the Chakra dimmed slightly, as though acknowledging his words. Then, with a final burst of brilliance, it vanished, leaving the clearing in silence.

Aftermath

The Nagas began to tend to their wounded, their movements calm and efficient. The Aghoris who had survived fled into the forest, their dark ambitions crushed by the very force they had sought to control.

Meera stood in stunned silence, her mind racing. She had witnessed something far beyond her understanding, a battle not just of bodies but of philosophies, of energies that shaped the very fabric of the universe.

Swami Shivananda approached her, his expression unreadable. "You have seen the truth, Meera. The Sudarshana Chakra is not just a relic of the past. It is the wheel of time, the force that ensures balance in an unbalanced world."

Meera nodded, her voice barely a whisper. "What happens now?"

Shivananda's gaze turned toward the horizon, where the first light of dawn was breaking. "The balance has been restored, for now. But our work is never done. The wheel of time turns, and the guardians must always remain vigilant."

CHAPTER SEVEN

The Eternal Vigil

The sun was climbing higher in the sky as the Sangam returned to its rhythm of devotion and ritual. But for Meera, the stillness felt unnatural, as if the echoes of the night's battle still lingered in the air. The forest behind her held secrets that would never be spoken, and the confluence ahead remained a silent witness to an eternal story of dharma and sacrifice.

The Nagas had won, yet the victory felt fragile, temporary, like a single breath in the cycle of life. Meera stood at the edge of the river, her fingers brushing against the rudraksha bead hanging around her neck. The air around her was filled with the distant hum of chants, but her mind was consumed by what she had seen.

A New Understanding of the Nagas

Later that morning, Meera approached Swami Shivananda, who was seated in meditation near the sacred fire. His stillness was remarkable, as though the battle of the previous night had left no mark on him. The other Nagas moved around the camp, their focus unwavering, as if the weight of their eternal task had already shifted back onto their shoulders.

"You've lived with this responsibility for centuries," Meera began softly, breaking the silence. "What drives you to keep going, knowing the battles will never end?"

Shivananda opened his eyes and looked at her with a calm intensity. "Dharma is not something that ends, Meera. It is not a goal or a destination, it is the eternal path. To walk that path is to accept the struggle as part of existence. We do not fight for victory; we fight for balance."

Meera sat down beside him, her curiosity tinged with reverence. "But what about the world? Most people don't even know what you do, or why."

"The world does not need to know," Shivananda replied. "The greatest acts of dharma are done in silence. The wheel of time turns regardless of whether anyone sees it, just as the Sudarshana Chakra spins, unseen, keeping the universe in harmony. Our task is to ensure that it continues."

The Sudarshana Chakra's Role in Kaliyuga

Meera's gaze drifted toward the horizon, where the faint glow of the Sangam reflected the light of the rising sun. "Swami-ji," she asked, her voice hesitant, "what happens if you fail? If the Chakra is ever taken?"

Shivananda's expression grew serious. "Kaliyuga is the age of shadows, where adharma thrives in disguise. If the Sudarshana Chakra were to fall into the wrong hands, it would unmake the balance of this age. The cycle of creation, preservation, and destruction would collapse, and chaos would consume the universe."

"But why does it remain in this world?" Meera pressed. "If it's so dangerous, why hasn't it been taken beyond reach?"

"Because the Sudarshana Chakra is not meant to be removed from creation," Shivananda explained. "It is the wheel of time itself, the essence of Sanatana Dharma. To remove it would be to remove the very fabric of existence. That is why it remains hidden, guarded not by walls or weapons, but by those who understand its true nature."

The Burden of the Guardians

Meera thought of Rudranath and the younger Nagas, their faces filled with a mixture of determination and weariness. "What about them?" she asked, gesturing toward the camp. "Do they ever question their path?"

"They are human, as you are," Shivananda said. "They feel doubt, fear, and longing, just as you do. But they have chosen this path because they know that dharma requires sacrifice. To guard the Chakra is to relinquish the self, to live not for oneself, but for the world."

He paused, his voice softening. "It is not an easy life, but it is a meaningful one. And meaning is what sustains us."

Meera's Decision

As the day wore on, Meera found herself standing at the edge of the Sangam once more. The sacred waters glittered under the sun, their currents carrying the prayers of millions. But Meera felt no need to make a wish or offer a prayer. She had seen what lay behind the veil of faith, the quiet, unrelenting work of those who held the universe together.

Rudranath approached her, his trident slung casually over his shoulder. "You're leaving soon, aren't you?"

Meera nodded. "I think it's time. But I'll never forget what I've seen here."

He smiled faintly. "You've witnessed what few ever will. Carry it with you, Meera. The world needs people who can remind it of what matters."

She touched the rudraksha bead around her neck. "I will."

The Wheel Turns

As Meera prepared to leave the Akhada, she turned back one last time. The Nagas were gathered around the central fire, their chants rising into the sky like a hymn to the cosmos:

"Shankaram Shankaracharyam Keshavam."

In that moment, Meera understood something she hadn't before. The Nagas were not just guardians of a divine artifact, they were custodians of an idea, a truth that had endured through every age. They were the silent flame that kept the wheel of time turning, ensuring that Sanatana Dharma would prevail, even in the darkest of times.

Epilogue: The Eternal Mystery

As the first light of dawn bathed the Sangam in gold, the Nagas began to scatter. Their movements were silent and deliberate, like shadows melting into the wilderness. One by one, they disappeared into the forest, leaving no trace of their presence save for the faint scent of burning incense and the lingering vibration of their chants.

Meera stood at the edge of the Akhada, watching as the ash-smeared warriors vanished into the horizon. She felt a strange mixture of awe and melancholy, knowing she would likely never see them again. For the Nagas did not linger, they had no homes, no attachments, no ties to the world they protected.

It was said that after every Kumbh, the Nagas retreated to the Himalayas, scattering themselves across its vast and secretive terrain. No one knew where they lived, how they communicated, or how they seemed to reappear, unified, at every Maha Kumbh. Their existence remained a puzzle, shrouded in secrecy for centuries. Even their physical appearance, their ash-covered bodies, their dreadlocked hair, their refusal to wear clothing, held meanings that no outsider could fully comprehend.

The Untold Secrets

Legends whispered that the Nagas were more than what they seemed, that their physical form was merely a vessel for something far greater. They did not fear the cold of the Himalayas, the scorching heat of the plains, or the trials of hunger and thirst, for their bodies were temples consecrated by the energy of the universe. The ash they smeared across their skin, drawn from sacred fires, was not just a symbol of renunciation but a shield of cosmic energy, marking them as warriors of the divine.

"Why do they live as they do?" Meera had once asked Swami Shivananda.

His response was simple yet profound. "Because to protect dharma, one must transcend the world. The Nagas renounce the physical not to escape life but to embody its deepest truths. The ash reminds us of what we are: dust, and to dust, we shall return."

The Vanishing Guardians

As Meera turned back toward the Sangam, she felt the weight of the Nagas' presence fading, like a dream slipping away upon waking. By the time the sun was fully risen, they were gone.

Some said the Nagas were messengers of the gods, descending only when dharma was at its most fragile. Others believed they were timeless souls, bound to this earth by a divine oath. But no one truly knew. And perhaps that was as it should be, for their greatest strength lay in their mystery.

Only one truth remained unshaken: when the world called, when dharma was threatened, the Nagas would return, appearing as suddenly as they had vanished, their chants echoing through the ages:

The Silent Wheel

Far away, deep in the Himalayan caves, the Sudarshana Chakra rested in its sanctuary, spinning gently, unseen by the world. Its golden glow pulsed with the rhythm of the cosmos, a silent testament to the balance it preserved. Around it, the air was still, yet alive with a divine energy.

No one knew where the Nagas kept their vigil. No one knew how they guarded the wheel of time. But the wheel turned, as it always had, and the guardians remained, eternal, unseen, and unyielding.

For the Nagas, life was not about being seen but about serving an eternal purpose. And in their vanishing, they left behind a truth that transcended words: that the protection of dharma required both sacrifice and mystery.

Author's Note

This book, *The Ash-Born Warriors*, is a work of fiction interwoven with elements of mythology, spirituality, and history. It is not a historical account, nor does it claim to present a definitive understanding of the Naga Sadhus, the Maha Kumbh, or the Sudarshana Chakra. Instead, it is a tribute to the timeless wisdom of Sanatana Dharma and the mysteries that continue to inspire generations.

The world we live in today is often consumed by chaos, confusion, and division. In such times, the essence of Sanatana Dharma, the eternal path, becomes all the more relevant. It is not merely a set of rituals or beliefs but a way of life that upholds balance, truth, and the interconnectedness of all existence. Sanatana Dharma reminds us that dharma, or righteous action, is the foundation of harmony in the universe.

Through this story, I sought to explore the unseen forces that strive to protect this balance, often at great personal sacrifice. The Naga Sadhus, enigmatic and misunderstood, symbolize the guardians of dharma, those who stand resolute against the tides of adharma, even when their work goes unnoticed or unacknowledged. Their renunciation of worldly attachments and their unwavering dedication to preserving cosmic harmony offer a profound lesson for all of us.

While the characters and events in this book are fictional, the ideals they represent are deeply rooted in the philosophy of Sanatana Dharma. The Sudarshana Chakra, as a symbol of cosmic order, serves as a reminder that balance is fragile and must be protected with vigilance and integrity.

This story is not just about the battles fought in the physical realm but also about the internal struggles we face as individuals. It invites readers to reflect on their own dharma, their own role in contributing to a world that honors truth, compassion, and justice.

As you close this book, I hope you carry with you a sense of wonder and reverence for the unseen forces that uphold our world. And I hope you are inspired to walk the path of dharma in your own way, *contributing to the legacy of Sanatana Dharma, the eternal flame that burns within us all.*

With gratitude,
YS Yadav
Author

About The Author

YS Yadav

Y.S.Yadav is a distinguished advocate, author, and social activist with an unwavering commitment to legal empowerment, social justice, and the preservation of cultural heritage. He practices law at the High Court of Andhra Pradesh and serves as the National President of Service Civil International (SCI-India), National Secretary of the Central Human Rights Organisation, National Executive Member of All India Yadav Mahasabha, and State Secretary of the Indian Association of Lawyers (IAL), Andhra Pradesh.

His passion for writing is evident in his diverse body of work, which spans the realms of law, history, and social reform. He has a unique ability to blend legal insights with compelling storytelling, making complex issues accessible and engaging for a wide range of readers. His published books include "The Constitution Speaks Stories of India's Top 25 Landmark. Judgments," "Golla Mandapam," "Gopika Geetham," "The YS Tales: Whispers of Wisdom" and

"When Gods Walked the Sacred Hills: LEGENDS OF SESHACHALAM. His upcoming works, "My Fate - A journey Beyond Boundaries and Beliefs" and "The Gambit of Gandhara," promise to be thought-provoking additions to his literary repertoire.

Beyond his legal and literary pursuits, Y.S. Yadav is a passionate advocate for the rights of marginalized communities, particularly the OBCs. He champions policy reforms, cultural heritage preservation, and social justice initiatives, striving to create a more equitable and inclusive society.

A firm believer in the mantra "Rise for Rights and Stand for Justice," his mission is to educate, empower, and inspire readers to engage with the law, history, and social issues that shape our world.

Thank You For Reading!

I hope The Ash-Born Warriors offered you not only an engaging journey into the world of the Naga Sadhus, the Maha Kumbh, and the Sudarshana Chakra but also a deeper understanding of the timeless principles of Sanatana Dharma.

Every story has a purpose, and this one was written to inspire reflection, curiosity, and reverence for the unseen forces that shape our existence. As the wheel of time continues to turn, let us all strive to walk the path of dharma, contributing to the balance and harmony of the universe in our own unique ways.

If this story resonated with you, I encourage you to share it with others. Discussions about our rich cultural and spiritual heritage are the first steps toward preserving it for generations to come.

May the flame of dharma continue to burn brightly in your life.

With gratitude and blessings,

Y.S. Yadav

Author of The Ash-Born Warriors